Timeless Quran Stories

The Story of the
Prophet Hud علیه السلام

SANIYASNAIN KHAN

goodwordbooks.com

Long time ago in the land of Yemen
there was a city called Iram.
Iram was a very big city.
The buildings were huge.
The gardens were very beautiful.
The people were very rich.

The people of Iram were proud.
They were proud of their city.
They were proud of their gardens.
They forgot that Allah gave them everything.
They forgot how to pray to Allah.
And they started to worship other gods.

There lived in the city of
Iram a man called Hud عليه السلام.
He was a prophet.
He loved Allah and prayed to Him.
He wanted other people also to
love Allah and pray to Him.

But they did not listen to him.
They turned their backs on him.
They were very proud and very arrogant.

The Prophet Hud ﷺ knew that Allah
does not like arrogant people.
He knew that Allah would punish them
if they did not change.
He knew that Allah would punish them
if they did not become good.

But people did not want to change.
They thought there is nothing
wrong with them.

Allah sent terrible drought
to punish them.
The wells went dry.
There was no water in the canals.
The green fields turned yellow.
Leaves dried and fell from the trees.
Flowers in the gardens
drooped their heads.
The animals cried with thirst.

The Prophet Hud ﷺ again warned the people.
He said: "Allah already punished you
with draught! Don't be wicked!
Allah will punish you more if you
don't listen!"
But people did not listen to him.

In the end Allah sent a terrible
wind to punish them more.
The terrible wind came riding on a
furious, dark cloud.
People saw the cloud coming
nearer and nearer.
They thought it was a rain cloud!
Their pride made them blind!
They did not see that it was the
terrible wind riding on a cloud.

They did not get it that
they were wrong.
They did not own up that
they were wicked!
They did not understand that
Allah did not like their wickedness!
The terrible wind blew for
seven nights and eight days.
The trees fell down with their
roots sticking up.

The houses were smashed.
The gardens were ruined.
The men were dead.
There was nothing left
of the city!
Allah saved only the Prophe[t]
Hud علیه السلام and the people
who listened to him.
Allah always saves those
who believe in Him!

Find Out More
To know more about the message and meaning of
Allah's words, look up the following parts of the
Quran which tell the story of the Prophet Hud علیه السلام.
Surah al-Araf 7:65-72
Surah Hud 11:50-60
Surah ash-Shuara 26:123-140
Surah al-Ahqaf 46:21-25

علیه السلام *Alayhis Salam* 'May peace be upon him.'
The customary blessings on the prophets.